Color Your Own
RENOIR
Paintings

Pierre-Auguste Renoir

Rendered by
Marty Noble

DOVER PUBLICATIONS, INC.
Mineola, New York

NOTE

Born at Limoges, France, Pierre-Auguste Renoir (1841–1919) was the son of a tailor, the sixth of seven children. In 1854, at thirteen, Renoir worked in a factory painting flowers onto porcelain dishes. At twenty-one, he enrolled at the École des Beaux-Arts and also entered Swiss artist Charles Gleyre's studio, where he met Alfred Sisley, Frédéric Bazille, and Claude Monet. These four art students, sharing a similar set of ideals regarding painting techniques, formed the core group of what would later become known as the Impressionists.

First exhibiting his works at the Salon in 1864, Renoir, along with Sisley, Bazille, and Monet, spent some time in the forest of Fontainebleau, painting landscapes directly from nature to study the effects of light, an act for which they were ridiculed by the more conservative mainstream artists running the Salons. Rejection by the Salons helped expedite plans for the first Impressionist exposition (1874), enabling a fresh group of painters, including Renoir, to gain visibility in the art world.

Renoir tended to paint portraits of women, children, and social scenes of everyday life since these were his favorite subjects. Using feathery brushstrokes and sparkling bursts of color, Renoir painted over two thousand portraits in his lifetime, some of which were commissions from publisher Georges Charpentier, who also organized an exhibition of Renoir's works in 1879 in the gallery La Vie Moderne. In 1881, Renoir traveled to Algeria and Italy, where he drew on Renaissance influences to break away from Impressionism and return to a classicism reminiscent of Raphael and Ingres. His series of *Bathers* executed at this time is a fine example of his extraordinary ability to portray the human form and its luminous qualities. After 1907, suffering from chronic rheumatism that robbed his fingers of their dexterity, Renoir had to paint with his brush tied to his hand.

All thirty of the paintings in this book are featured in full color on the front and back covers. Use this color scheme as a guide to create your own adaptation of a Renoir or change the colors to see the effects of color and tone on each painting. Captions identify the title of the work, date of composition, medium employed, and the size of the original painting.

Bibliographical Note

Color Your Own Renoir Paintings is a new work, first published by Dover Publications, Inc., in 2001.

DOVER *Pictorial Archive* SERIES

This book belongs to the Dover Pictorial Archive Series. You may use the designs and illustrations for graphics and crafts applications, free and without special permission, provided that you include no more than four in the same publication or project. (For permission for additional use, please write to Permissions Department, Dover Publications, Inc., 31 East 2nd Street, Mineola, N.Y. 11501.)
However, republication or reproduction of any illustration by any other graphic service, whether it be in a book or in any other design resource, is strictly prohibited.

International Standard Book Number: 0-486-41546-5

Manufactured in the United States of America
Dover Publications, Inc., 31 East 2nd Street, Mineola, N.Y. 11501

1. **Madame Charpentier with Her Children.** 1878. Oil on canvas. 64½ x 74⅛ in. (153.6 x 190 cm.)

2. **Portrait of Romaine Lacaux.** 1864. Oil on canvas. 31¾ x 25½ in. (81 x 65 cm.)

3. **Spring Bouquet.** 1866. Oil on canvas. 39½ x 31 in. (101 x 79 cm.)

4. Alfred Sisley and His Wife. 1868. Oil on canvas. 41½ x 29 in. (106 x 74 cm.)

5. **The Box ("La Loge").** 1874. Oil on canvas. 31½ x 24 in. (80 x 63 cm.)

6. **Portrait of the Actress Jeanne Samary.** 1878. Oil on canvas. 68 x 40½ in. (173 x 103 cm.)

7. **Two Little Circus Girls.** 1879. Oil on canvas. 51½ x 39 in. (131.5 x 99.5 cm.)

8. **After the Meal.** 1879. Oil on canvas. 39$\frac{1}{16}$ x 32$\frac{1}{4}$ in. (99.5 x 82 cm.)

9. **Woman with a Fan.** 1881. Oil on canvas. 25½ x 19¾ in. (65 x 50 cm.)

10. **Pink and Blue: Alice and Elisabeth Cahen d'Anvers.** 1881. Oil on canvas. $46\frac{5}{8}$ x $29\frac{1}{8}$ in. (119 x 74 cm.)

11. **On the Terrace.** 1881. Oil on canvas. $39\frac{3}{8}$ x $31\frac{1}{2}$ in. (100 x 80 cm.)

12. **Charles and Georges Durand-Ruel.** 1882. Oil on canvas. 25⅝ x 31⅞ in. (65 x 81 cm.)

13. **Luncheon of the Boating Party.** 1880–1881. Oil on canvas. 51¼ x 68⅛ in. (130 x 173 cm.)

14. Dance in the Country. 1882–1883. Oil on canvas. 70⅞ x 35⅜ in. (180 x 90 cm.)

15. **Dance in the City.** 1882–1883. Oil on canvas. 70⅞ x 35⅜ in. (180 x 90 cm.)

16. **The Umbrellas.** ca. 1881/1885. Oil on canvas. 70¾ x 45¼ in. (180 x 115 cm.)

17. **Seated Bather.** ca. 1883–1884. Oil on canvas. 47¾ x 35¾ in. (121 x 91 cm.)

18. **Chrysanthemums in a Vase.** ca. 1884. Oil on canvas. $31\frac{7}{8}$ x $25\frac{5}{8}$ in. (81 x 65 cm.)

19. **By the Seashore.** 1883. Oil on canvas. 36¼ x 28¾ in. (92 x 73 cm.)

20. **The Children's Afternoon at Wargemont.** 1884. Oil on canvas. 50 x 68 in. (127 x 173 cm.)

21. **Mont Sainte-Victoire.** 1888–1889. Oil on canvas. 20⅞ x 25¼ in. (53 x 64 cm.)

22. **Girl with a Hoop (Marie Goujon).** 1885. Oil on canvas. 49½ x 30⅛ in. (125.7 x 76.6 cm.)

23. **Child with a Whip (Étienne Goujon).** 1885. Oil on canvas. 41⅞ x 29½ in. (105 x 75 cm.)

24. **Gladioli.** ca. 1885. Oil on canvas. 29½ x 21⅜ in. (75 x 54.5 cm.)

25. **Julie Manet with a Cat.** 1887. Oil on canvas. 25½ x 21 in. (64.5 x 53.5 cm.)

26. **Jean Playing with Gabrielle and a Girl.** 1895–1896. Oil on canvas. 25⅝ x 31½ in. (65 x 80 cm.)

27. **Yvonne and Christine Lerolle at the Piano.** 1897. Oil on canvas. 28³/₄ x 36¹/₄ in. (73 x 92 cm.)

28. **Girls at the Piano.** 1892. Oil on canvas. 45½ x 35½ in. (116 x 90 cm.)

29. **Woman with a Guitar.** 1896–1897. Oil on canvas. 31¾ x 25⅝ in. (81 x 65 cm.)

30. Self-Portrait. ca. 1899. Oil on canvas. 16 x 13 in. (41 x 33 cm.)